THE CHURCH
OF
THE POISONED
MIND

The Church of the Poisoned Mind

Published by:
VJ PUBLISHINGHOUSE, LLC.
20451 NW 2nd Avenue Suite112 Miami Gardens, Fl. 33169   Phone:786-535-9598/786-303-9551
www.vjpublishinghouse.com
vjpublishinghouse@gmail.com

ISBN: 978-1-939236-09-8

©Copyright: 2024, March
Luis H. Alvarado
All Rights Reserved:

No portion of this book or any digital products may be reproduced, stored, in any retrieval system, or transmitted by any means without the written consent of Author except in reviews or articles with Author consent or as permitted by U.S. copyright law.

Go ye into all the world and preach the gospel to every creature.

DEDICATION

This book is dedicated to my first teachers of the gospel and spiritual warfare.

Overseer: Sarah J. Isom-Murray
And
Valerie D. Spann-Johnson

Founders of "The Warriors for Christ Bible Band"
Established in 1980 at Fort Riley, Kansas

Sarah J. Isom-Murray and Valerie D. Spann-Johnson

ACKNOWLEDGMENTS

First and foremost, I give thanks to the Most-High God, to my Savior Jesus Christ, and my helper and leader, the Holy Ghost.

To my wife Denise, whom I have the pleasure of loving with all my heart. Thank you, Sweetie, for putting up with me.

To my sons, Luis M, Jose J, and Isaac J. To my one and only daughter, Lily J. I love you all dearly and am so very proud of each one of you.

To my parents who have gone to glory, the late Juan R. and Concepcion Alvarado, I miss you two dearly.

To my brothers, the late Jose J. Alvarado, Carlos E. Alvarado and my sisters, Julia E., Curry, Vanessa Brilliant, and the late Iris D. Jones.

To a host of family and friends over my lifetime, I love you all, and Blessings Always!!!

To the readers of this book, thank you for your support. I pray that you find the peace of God, which surpasses all understanding, as you journey on in this life so that you may hear, **"WELL DONE THOU GOOD & FAITHFUL SERVANT."**

TABLE OF CONTENTS

Page 1 ………………………………………………….. Introduction

Page 5 …………………………………………………… Chapter 1

Page 11……………………………………………………. Chapter 2

Page 23 …………………………………………………… Chapter 3

Page 29…………………………………………………... Chapter 4

Page 33 ……………………………………………… … Chapter 5

Page 37…………………………………………………... Chapter 6

Page 43 …………………………………………………...Chapter 7

Page 49 …………………………………………………. Chapter 8

Page 53 ………………………………………………… Chapter 9

Page 59…………………………………………………. Chapter 10

Page 63 …………………………………………………….Epilogue

~Introduction~

Seeing the state of The Church over the past 20-plus years and the decline of True Worshippers attending year after year, I embarked upon writing by the unction and leading of The Holy Spirit to examine, according to The Holy Scriptures, this declination. This book is not intended to single out any one particular denomination, group of believers, or any single ministry. What this book will attempt to explain is, over the past 20 or so years, how the church has seemed to have lost its place as the place where people collectively come together to commune with their God. There seems to have been a transformation, whereas once upon a time, The Church was looked upon and respected as The House of God. Nowadays, any and everything that once was frowned upon by believers is now welcomed and reverence in The House of God.

How did it happen, and what will be the path to restoring The House of God to its position on earth as **"THE BRIDE OF CHRIST?"** We'll examine scriptures to see how God sees **THE HOUSE OF GOD.**

The Church of The Poisoned Mind is only the author's point of view, and again, no particular ministry, denomination, leader, or place of Worship is intended to be singled out. The poison has been injected since the inception of the early churches and has been passed through the bloodstream from generation to generation. I ask only for your prayers that this book shines a light in dark places of all our lives and brings an understanding of how we, as a people worldwide, have lost a hunger for God, the creator of all things.

Whether you're a believer or not, we all will stand before Him, whether to be welcomed or to hear the words **"DEPART FROM ME!"**

KEY SCRIPTURES:

1 Timothy 4:1-3 *(King James Version)*

4 Now the Spirit speaketh expressly, that in the latter times, some shall depart from the faith, giving heed to seducing spirits, and doctrines of devils.

2 Speaking lies in hypocrisy; having their conscience seared with a hot iron; Forbidding to marry, and commanding to abstain from meats, which God hath created to be received with thanksgiving of them which believe and know the truth.

2 Timothy 4 *(King James Version)*

4 I charge thee therefore before God, and the Lord Jesus Christ, who shall judge the quick and the dead at his appearing and his kingdom. Preach the word; be instant in season, out of season; reprove, rebuke, exhort with all long-suffering and doctrine.

For the time will come when they will not endure sound doctrine; but after their own lusts shall they heap to themselves teachers, having itching ears; And they shall turn away their ears from the truth and shall be turned unto fables.

2 Thessalonians 2 *(King James Version)*

2 Now we beseech you, brethren, by the coming of our Lord Jesus Christ, and by our gathering together unto him,

That ye be not soon shaken in mind, or be troubled, neither by Spirit, nor by word, nor by letter as from us, as that the day of Christ is at hand.

Let no man deceive you by any means: for that day shall not come, except there comes a falling away first, and that man of sin be revealed, the son of perdition. 4 Who opposeth and exalteth himself above all that is called God, or that is worshipped; so that he as God sitteth in the temple of God, showing himself that he is God.

Even him, whose coming is after the working of Satan with all power and signs and lying wonders,

And with all deceivableness of unrighteousness in them that perish; because they received not the love of the truth, that they might be saved.

And for this cause, God shall send them strong delusion, that they should believe a lie:

That they all might be damned who believed not the truth but had pleasure in unrighteousness.

CHURCH: *noun*

The ecclesiastical government of a particular religious group or its power, and the people who attend or make up the church (members).

Poison: A substance that can cause illness or death when eaten, drunk, or absorbed, even in relatively small quantities.

Anything harmful or destructive to happiness or welfare, such as an emotion or idea.

To influence wrongfully, corrupt (to poison one's mind).

~CHAPTER 1~
The Warnings

The Apostle Paul, in his writings or epistles, gives us words that encourage, enlighten, teach, warn, and rebuke. Paul warns us about a coming that has already begun infiltrating our churches, homes, and, if we're not watchful, our minds.

Paul alerts us in II Thessalonians 2: 3-4

"Let no man deceive you by any means." Understand what the Apostle Paul is saying.

"ANY MEANS!" No matter what, let no man deceive you.

1Timothy 4:1 alerts us, "Now the Spirit speaketh expressly, that in the latter times, some shall depart from the faith, giving heed to seducing spirits, and doctrines of devils.

Not only that, but II Timothy 4: 3-4 also warns us, "**3** For the time will come when they will not endure sound doctrine; but after their own lusts shall they heap to themselves teachers, having itching ears; **4** And they shall turn away their ears from the truth, and shall be turned unto fables.

And what is a fable? Simply put, a fable is a story that is not true, a falsehood, A LIE!!

II Thessalonians 2: 9-12, Paul makes it clear that "**9** Even him, whose coming is after the working of Satan with all power and signs and lying wonders,

And with all deceivableness of unrighteousness in them that perish; because they received not the love of the truth, that they might be saved. And for this cause God shall send them strong delusion, that they should believe a lie:
That they all might be damned who believed not the truth but had pleasure in unrighteousness.

Now, this is the church of the poisoned mind! Amen & Amen! The Bible speaks of these things to come in the latter times, the last days. My brothers and sisters, let me submit that those days are upon us now, even as we sit here reading this book. Many have come with a new message that is not according to the Word of God. A message that will take you from the straight and narrow and put you on the broad wide highway that is traveled by many, so says **St Matthew 7: 13** Enter ye in at the strait gate: for wide is the gate, and broad is the way, that leadeth to destruction, and many there be which go in there at:
14 Because strait is the gate, and narrow is the way, which leadeth unto life, and few there be that find it. And how is it that many are being led this way?

In II Timothy 4:2, Paul commands us to "preach the word; be instant in season, out of season; reprove, rebuke, exhort with all long-suffering and doctrine." Preach: to declare, to proclaim in public.

Reprove means to express disapproval of something said or done. In other words, if it isn't in line with God's Word, it's not the truth. Rebuke: blame or scold sharply meaning put the spotlight on it to reveal the falsehood. Not quietly icing it over so it doesn't offend or hurt someone's feelings. It is supposed to be sharp, and we know that anything sharp is liable to cut, stab, puncture, or cause pain. In the old days, when someone had cancer and went into the hospital for surgery, the doctors would cut the cancerous area away from the noncancerous organs to keep it from spreading to the entire body, preventing it from causing significant pain and eventual death. To get the poison out of the minds of the church, one has to rebuke that that isn't of God.

How will we know what is the truth from the poison?

The Apostle Paul instructs us in **II Timothy 2:5,** Study to shew thyself approved unto God, a workman that needed not to be ashamed, rightly dividing the word of truth.

This is the only way to know the truth. Again, let no man deceive you by any means.

Know the Word of God for yourself and trust it to be your road map to The Kingdom of God. You can ask for directions from others, but if they need to become more familiar with the area, they can only direct you in what they think is the way. Not everybody is familiar with the TRUE Word of GOD. It takes a willingness on one's behalf to study and pray for understanding of what The Spirit is saying through the scriptures. No, not one person knows it all, but according to God's will for one's life, the scriptures will reveal the truth. Some are not prepared to know the truth, for in knowing the truth, one's life is subject to change. The truth will reveal oneself first and where one stands in their relationship with God. Are we willing to correct ourselves first and foremost for His will to be revealed in our lives? Yes, only God knows you, the real you. The one you hide from others, the one who secretly cries out for answers to your life. The one who thinks their wrongdoings are invisible for others to see, but God sees it all.

~CHAPTER 2~
IT'S LATER THAN YOU THINK

The Church of The Poisoned Mind is already at work. It started ages ago. There was a time when the gospel was preached and taught straight from the Bible, and we learned about the beginning, the fall of man, the devil, and God's plan of redemption, which is the life, death, and resurrection from the dead of Jesus Christ. Somewhere, the gospel had begun to be watered down to fit one's personal belief, and then came the false teachings. Now, this didn't happen suddenly, but with a small dose of false teaching (thus the poison), we accepted that dose because it made us feel better about our condition, not realizing that it was poison.

Many who once believed in God and preached the truth now preach a different message. They believe in same-sex marriages, and people with alternative lifestyles are now allowed not only to stay in that lifestyle but have been given positions and titles and even hold leadership offices in different capacities within the church. The preaching of being saved from sin is a forgotten message in some churches. The theme now is to be politically correct and not offend anyone. The fear of losing membership, losing finances, and being branded a fire and brimstone preacher has contributed to the spreading of the poison throughout the body of Christ. These false teachings are attributed to the belief that God is an all-loving and merciful God and that He will not utterly destroy the wickedness that's been running rampant throughout the earth. Many believe that when Jesus returns, He will return as a loving Savior, and everybody will be accepted into the Kingdom of Heaven. He came the first time as The Lamb of God, loving, caring, forgiving, teaching, and preaching the Kingdom of God is at hand. Yet we received Him not. We turned our backs to The Word of God and kept on living as though God never existed and we were our own savior. The poison only led to further deceive us into thinking that there's no truth in The Gospel. We were lured into a false sense of security, feeling that there is no God, and if there is, then we limit Him to our perspective and not see Him as who He is.

We cannot limit an unlimited God to our perspectives, therefore making ourselves our own God.

John 4:23-25 *(King James Version)*

But the hour cometh, and now is, when the true worshippers shall worship the Father in Spirit and in truth: for the Father seeketh such to worship him.

God is a Spirit: and they that worship him must worship him in Spirit and in truth. This passage of scripture teaches us that the hour is upon us when true worshippers shall worship The Father in Spirit and in truth, for the Father seeketh those to worship Him.

Who are the true worshippers? Those who have not been defiled or poisoned by the world. Jesus laid out what real, true Worship is; first, it's **to worship God in Spirit and truth**. That means you understand who God is and all about the Godhead. So authentic Worship is more than singing songs; real Worship involves what Romans says, "your body as a living sacrifice."

What are the elements of true Worship?

4 Elements of Genuine Worship

• Worship is wonderment. As Isaiah enters the presence of God, he is awestruck by God's majesty and Holiness.

Isaiah 6 *(King James Version)*

6 In the year that King Uzziah died, I saw also the Lord sitting upon a throne, high and lifted up, and his train filled the temple.

Above it stood the seraphims: each one had six wings; with twain, he covered his face, and with twain, he covered his feet, and with twain, he did fly.

And one cried unto another and said, Holy, holy, holy, is the Lord of hosts: the whole earth is full of his glory.

And the posts of the door moved at the voice of him that cried, and the house was filled with smoke.

Then said I, Woe is me! for I am undone; because I am a man of unclean lips, and I dwell in the midst of a people of unclean lips: for mine eyes have seen the King, the Lord of hosts.

Then flew one of the seraphims unto me, having a live coal in his hand, which he had taken with the tongs from off the altar:

And he laid it upon my mouth, and said, Lo, this hath touched thy lips; and thine iniquity is taken away, and thy sin purged.

Also, I heard the voice of the Lord, saying, Whom shall I send, and who will go for us? Then said I, Here am I; send me.

And he said, Go, and tell this people, Hear ye indeed, but understand not; and see ye indeed, but perceive not.

Worship is transformative. In his experience of God's presence, Isaiah sees who he really is – a sinner…

Worship is renewing…

We see here that the Prophet Isaiah was awestruck by God's glory when in God's presence. He recognized that being in God's presence, he found himself to be a man of unclean lips, and he dwelled among the same kind of people.

There's more to worship than, as the saying goes, "I'M GETTING MY PRAISE ON." True Worship causes one to see oneself as they really are before God: "UNCLEAN." It will cause us to recognize the sovereignty of God and recognize that we're unclean. But the time is now when the true worshippers shall worship the Father in Spirit and in truth.

True Worship is not for entertainment, getting our praise on, or being recognized as a soloist, instrument player, or choir director. We must come bowed down and surrender to God's will. When we forget or don't acknowledge God as the one and only True God, we will end up in the Lake of Fire.

As time is spent, we've witnessed the laws changing in the political arena because they have their own agenda. It's been told over and over, but because of the minute doses of poison we've been given throughout our lifetime, we feel as though nothing's going to happen. Our adversary has been very clever and subtle in launching deceptive poisoning over the years. You see, they only administer doses too small to notice to the worldly mind, and we begin to accept that whatever the world says is the truth is truth. Lulling us to a false sense of safety. They test the doses amongst the human race to see how much resistance and where the resistance is coming from. When resistance is detected, a readjustment of poison is administered to those who oppose the world and flesh.

Pitting one against another. Race, gender, religious belief, social status, political status, and the list goes on and on, so much so that it has infiltrated the church and poisoned the minds of many. Causing denominational disagreements, infighting within denominations, and believing a lie over the truth.

1 Timothy 4 *(King James Version)*

4 Now the Spirit speaketh expressly, that in the latter times some shall depart from the faith, giving heed to seducing spirits, and doctrines of devils.

2 Speaking lies in hypocrisy; having their conscience seared with a hot iron; 3 Forbidding to marry, and commanding to abstain from meats, which God hath created to be received with thanksgiving of them which believe and know the truth.

The poison has caused some to depart from the FAITH and TRUTH. Heeding to the poison that has been slowly entering their spiritual blood system, changing their spiritual DNA from a Holy Father to the lying devil, calling truth a lie and lie, the truth. This slow process of administering the poison has seduced those who once believed in Holiness to believe lies. The preaching of the gospel to the entertainment of the crowds. Mega Churches were on the rise at one point when I first began writing this book. Suddenly, Mega Churches were the in thing. Thousands would flock to them, seeking not the presence of God but to be amongst the number. Many gave themselves into the atmosphere that these Mega Churches offered, but

there was no transforming nor renewing taking place. Just like they sprung up, these Mega
Churches began to decline because, for the most part, God's presence wasn't there.

Oh, there was preaching, dancing, prophecies, laying on of hands, and all, but the Word of God that changes lives didn't prevail. Yes, the membership grew, and the finances bloomed, but Holiness didn't stick to the minds of those who flocked to these Mega Churches. I'm not against Mega Churches, but I believe that when God's presence is in the midst, lives are changed, and continuing in The Word, even after attending any Church, we should strengthen our faith. But just like a good movie, sporting event, or concert, after the excitement of attending, once the event is over, so is our zeal to continue in our daily Worship and study of The Word of God.

Not only is the toxin of the minds evident in our church, but it is everywhere you go in our government. Our government leaders are coming out of the closet about their womanizing lifestyles, their homosexual lifestyles, and other lifestyles that are an abomination unto God. Yet they are in charge of running our country, making decisions that will affect us all. These are the latter days. (Already in the works are the small chips and other devices to be implanted into one's person so that they may be able to control our every move. It's being played out right before our eyes.

How can we consider ourselves to be Holy and yet ignore the signs in place?

2 Corinthians 2:1-11 Lest Satan should get an advantage of us: for we are not ignorant of his devices.

Let's open our eyes and see what's happening in the world and what the Spirit says unto us. Let's take heed and be sensitive to The Holy Spirit.

As Jesus said in **St John 14:26**

26 But the Comforter, which is the Holy Ghost, whom the Father will send in my name, shall teach you all things, and bring all things to your remembrance, whatsoever I have said unto you.

I John 2: 26-27 echoes the exact words:

26 These things have I written unto you concerning them that seduce you. 27 But the anointing which ye have received of him abideth in you, and ye need not that any man teach you: but as the same anointing teacheth you of all things, and is truth, and is no lie, and even as it hath taught you, ye shall abide in him.

The Holy Ghost which the Spirit of Truth, shall lead us into all truth if we allow Him to. Let no man deceive you by any means. We must be in prayer and fasting, being watchful at all times. Just look at the economy and how it's getting worse. Prices have increased so much that it's difficult for many to keep up. Thus, setting up what **Revelations** speaks about in the **13th chapter, verses 11-18:**

And I beheld another beast coming up out of the earth, and he had two horns like a lamb, and he spake as a dragon.
And he exerciseth all the power of the first beast before him, and causeth the earth and them which dwell therein to worship the first beast, whose deadly wound was healed.
And he doeth great wonders, so that he maketh fire come down from heaven on the earth in the sight of men,
And deceiveth them that dwell on the earth by the means of those miracles which he had power to do in the sight of the beast; saying to them that dwell on the earth, that they should make an image to the beast, which had the wound by a sword, and did live.
And he had power to give life unto the image of the beast, that the image of the beast should both speak, and cause that as many as would not worship the image of the beast should be killed.
And he causeth all, both small and great, rich, and poor, free and bond, to receive a mark in their right hand, or in their foreheads:
And that no man might buy or sell, save he that had the mark, or the name of the beast, or the number of his name.

Here is wisdom. Let him that hath understanding count the number of the beast: for it is the number of a man, and his number is Six hundred three-score and six.

This system has been in place for many years, and they've been working on perfecting it. The necessities for survival are becoming far too expensive to afford houses, transportation, gas, food, clothing, and more.

Paul admonishes us in **Ephesians 6:10**

Finally, my brethren, be strong in the Lord, and in the power of his might.

Put on the whole armor of God, that ye may be able to stand against the wiles of the devil.

For we wrestle not against flesh and blood, but against principalities, against powers, against the rulers of the darkness of this world, against spiritual wickedness in high places.

This is our wake-up call to prepare ourselves for the battle already underway. It began after Jesus's resurrection. The powers of darkness realized that they could not hold our Lord. Being justified and glorified by His Father, Jesus couldn't remain in the grave.

WAKE UP PEOPLE! WAKE UP!

~CHAPTER 3~
THE COST OF SIN

In **Romans 6:23-** For the wages of sin is death; but the gift of God is eternal life through Jesus Christ our Lord.

The church of the poisoned mind would have you believe this is untrue. How can a God who loves us all turn around and destroy what He loves? Yes, God does love us; however, it's the sin that has overcome us, like cancer. Destroying all of what God has placed within our being from the beginning. God hates sin, and sin cannot inherit The Kingdom of God. Therefore, once again, let no man deceive you by any means. For the day of The Lord comes as a thief in the night. It doesn't take long for a thief to steal all your belongings when you're not being watchful. A thief can get into your house and steal away your livelihood within a matter of minutes. He doesn't go in blindly; he watches and observes your coming and going from your home. A thief knows when your home is vulnerable. Once he figures out your weakness, he will strike. The moment you least expect, then BOOM, the damage is done.

If we don't keep our minds steadfast on Jesus and put Him first in all we do, we give space to the devil to learn our vulnerabilities. He then plans his attack to get into our minds and steal what we know to be the truth. He comes subtle at first, not to cause an alarm in your Spirit. His talk sounds good, and yes, it may make sense, but don't believe the hype!

Know that The Holy Spirit works in your life and allow Him to lead and guide you in truth. If you don't have The Holy Spirit on the inside, then "GET HIM!" The Holy Spirit is like a 24-hour spiritual guard and is on duty to protect you from thieves. No other security system in the world can protect you like The Holy Spirit. Some of us spend our well-earned money on ADT, BRINKS, and other systems for our homes, cars, and workplaces. These alarms are known to have failures and need to be replaced with an upgrade that will cost us even more. The Holy Spirit never fails or needs upgrading. The Holy Spirit is a sure thing and only costs us time. Time in prayer, fasting, and studying God's Word. Time in Worship and praise, fellowship, and even time alone with God. These times, when spent wisely, will keep us before the presence of God so that we have no wanting to sin within us because sin cannot dwell in His presence. Where there is no sin (in His presence), there is no wages for it, meaning no death but life everlasting. Pray for the Holy Spirit to dwell in you if you have not received the gift promised to all who believe. The Prophet Joel prophesied in:

Joel 2:28 *(King James)*

And it shall come to pass afterward, that I will pour out my Spirit upon all flesh; and your sons and your daughters shall prophesy, your old men shall dream dreams, your young men shall see visions:

29 And also upon the servants and upon the handmaids in those days will I pour out my Spirit.

The promise came to pass in **The Book of Acts**

2:1 And when the day of Pentecost was fully come, they were all with one accord in one place.

And suddenly there came a sound from heaven as of a rushing mighty wind, and it filled all the house where they were sitting.

And there appeared unto them cloven tongues like as of fire, and it sat upon each of them.

And they were all filled with the Holy Ghost and began to speak with other tongues, as the Spirit gave them utterance.

The fulfillment is available for all who believe even today. The gift is ours for the asking. The Holy Spirit is our help and our way to be caught up!   Disobedience to God's word is sin, and that will cost us eternal life in Christ Jesus.

2 Timothy 4 *(King James Version)*

4 I charge thee therefore before God, and the Lord Jesus Christ, who shall judge the quick and the dead at his appearing and his kingdom. Preach the word; be instant in season, out of season; reprove, rebuke, exhort with all long-suffering and doctrine.

For the time will come when they will not endure sound doctrine; but after their own lusts shall they heap to themselves teachers, having itching ears. And they shall turn away their ears from the truth and shall be turned unto fables. 5 But watch thou in all things, endure afflictions, do the work of an evangelist, make full proof of thy ministry.

They will not endure sound doctrine. In other words, the truth. Many will start zealously for God and want to do His will, but the lack of prayer, fasting, and studying will cause them to get comfortable in one place and not maintain their hunger for God. Don't allow your hunger to be satisfied with the things of this world but be filled with The Spirit of God and an everlasting hunger to know Him even more daily. We must have the will to keep God first and foremost in our lives and not give space for the poison to creep into our spirits.

Whenever we set out to achieve a specific goal, we study the requirements, applications, time, place, and sacrifices we must make to obtain our goals. If we begin to think it's impossible from the start, then it will be so. But if we plan how to achieve our goals step by step, we can conquer them and remain hungry for the next step. An athlete doesn't give up on their first attempt. Sometimes, it takes many failures before they can determine what and how to overcome and complete their goal. Never give up, nor give in. A winner never quits, and a quitter never wins. Glory Hallelujah, You're a winner! Eternal life awaits you when you live for Jesus, and you will bypass the wages of sin.

~CHAPTER 4~
THE BEGINNING

"THE FIRST POISONING"

Genesis 1st and 2nd chapters of the scriptures tell us how God created the heavens and the earth. The earth was without form and void. The Spirit of God moved, and as God spoke, things began to take shape. In six days, the lights, the heavens, the seas, and every creature therein, the dry lands, the grass, trees, and all creatures upon the earth. Man after His image. Male and female. God blessed them and said to be fruitful and multiply. All that God made, He said, was good. And on the 7th day, God rested from all His work which He made.

After creating man and woman, God put them in a garden that He Himself had planted. (EDEN) This garden had three rivers that flowed throughout it. There were trees in this garden, which provided food for man and woman. God instructed man on how to manage the garden and that he should not eat from one tree, the tree of knowledge of good and evil, for he would surely die. God Himself issued the first warning of the poisoning.

In the **3rd chapter of Genesis,** the Bible introduces us to the serpent- the originator of the poison. It describes this being as more subtle than any beast God made. Webster's Dictionary gives us several direct meanings of the word subtle. It defines subtle as 1) capable of making or noticing fine distinctions in meaning. 2) Requiring mental keenness. 3) delicately skillful or clever: deft or ingenious. 4) delicately suggestive, not grossly obvious, not easily detected. All of these meanings are wrapped up in the conversation that transpired between the serpent and the woman. First, the serpent said unto the woman, "Yea hath

God hath said, ye shall eat of every tree of the garden? Who is the serpent to question what God has already established between Himself and man?

In Revelation 12:9

9 And the great dragon was cast out, that old serpent, called the devil, and Satan, which deceiveth the whole world: he was cast out into the earth, and his angels were cast out with him.

The devil is called Satan. He's also known as Lucifer. He once dwelled in heaven with God. Somehow, Lucifer thought to himself and said within his heart.

Isaiah 14:12-14 *(King James Version)*

How art thou fallen from heaven, O Lucifer, son of the morning! How art thou cut down to the ground, which didst weaken the nations!

For thou hast said in thine heart, I will ascend into heaven, I will exalt my throne above the stars of God: I will also sit upon the mount of the congregation, in the sides of the north.

He thought to make himself better than God. This was his first poisoning, which he administered to himself. His plan backfired, and he and a third of the angels who rebelled with him were cast out of heaven. He rebelled and influenced many angels to believe his poison. Thus, the first poisoning occurred in heaven, and upon his arrival to earth, he had a new name (Satan), which means the accuser, adversary, slanderer, now set his eyes on the very creation of God.

Notice how he begins questioning the woman concerning every tree in the garden. He suggests that it's okay to eat from every tree in the garden. The woman replies, "We may eat of the fruit of the trees but of the fruit of the tree which is in the midst of the garden. God said, Ye shall not eat of it neither shall ye touch it, lest ye die". The serpent responded, "Ye shall not surely die." Knowing that the woman didn't realize why he made such a statement, he didn't allow her to think about it but implied that God knows that the day you eat from it, your eyes shall be opened and be as gods knowing good and evil. This statement made the woman rethink what she had been instructed about this tree, and the thought of being a god was more appealing to her than obedience. It causes her to look at the tree differently. Don't allow false doctrines to cause you to look at The Word of God differently than what it is. The serpent was set on destroying God's creation by any means possible. He introduced suggestive thoughts to the woman, and she did the thought along with the idea of being a god. Once that thought was received, she reacted physically by eating the fruit. This was the first poisoning on the earth. God cursed the serpent, above all, the beast of the field, and commanded him to go upon his belly and eat dust for the rest of his life. Can you imagine that? He may like the dust because he's trying to devour all mankind, which came from the dust. Judgment was also declared upon the man and woman. Poison destroys and does not discriminate, nor does it have respect of persons. **STAY WOKE PEOPLE!**

~CHAPTER 5~
A POISONING THAT LED TO MURDER
(Genesis 4:1-6)

Adam and Eve bore their first two sons, Cain, and Abel. Now, Cain was a tiller of the ground. The problem that Cain was facing was that he toiled in the very ground that God had cursed. His work was hard and tedious. Abel, on the other hand, was a keeper of sheep. He cared for his sheep. Now, there came a time when sacrifices were brought before God. Cain brought fruit from the ground, and Abel brought his firstlings and the fat. This means Abel brought the best of his flock before God as an offering. And God respected Abel's offering and Abel also. But unto Cain and his offering, God had no respect. God cursed the ground, and God would not accept what was cursed. Cain was outraged. Anger is a feeling of displeasure and the intent to fight back the cause of it. In this case, Cain felt anger for not having his offering accepted by God. God asked Cain why art thou wroth? Why are you angry? God told Cain that if he did well, He would accept his offering, but if he didn't, that sin lay at the door. Learn to close all portals which will cause us to sin.

In other words, temptation will attempt to poison our minds and cause us to sin. Cain didn't heed God's warning, but he allowed himself to be tempted. Only it was his brother Abel who would fall to the poison of Cain's mind. Abel had no idea what Cain was about to do. Cain's anger kindled against his brother Abel. It was not Abel's fault that God was not pleased with Cain's offering. Nevertheless, Abel would pay the ultimate price for being Blessed by God. How many times have you seen this very poison on our jobs, homes, and churches? Someone is recognized for a job well done, and the poison begins to creep into the minds of those not recognized. The plot to make that person pay is often planted. Whether it's to discredit one's achievement or to bring the skeletons out of the closets of church leaders and laypeople alike, no one is immune to this poison unless you protect yourself against it. Our protection against this poison is PRAYER, FASTING, STUDYING God's Word, and having The Holy Spirit indwelling to lead and guide us to the truth.

Many have fallen victim to such poisoning because they did not heed the warnings. Envy, jealousy, strife, pride, wickedness, hatred, and anger. These are just some of the poisonings that can destroy not only our peace of mind but also those whom we love and care for. The results of poisoning can be lethal. Is there an antidote?

~CHAPTER 6~
THE TARGET OF THE POISON (THE MIND)

The poison we speak of targets specific areas in our bodies, particularly the mind and the heart. The poisoning that is administered to the mind is so subtle that our mind gradually becomes immune to it. It's not overpowering enough to activate our defense mechanism immediately. Little by little, it seeps and creeps in undetected- undetected by those of us who don't study to show ourselves approved unto God, pray, or fast, or allow the Holy Spirit to lead and guide us.

The mind, if we could use Webster's Dictionary as a point of reference, is defined as:

1) that which thinks, perceives, feels, will, etc.

2) the intellect in its normal state.

Intellect is the ability to reason or understand the power of thought. Now, we have intellect, power, perception, understanding, feelings, thinking, and will. All are vital to the operation of the mind. Yet Webster acknowledges that all these functions are in their normal state. A healthy mind is a normal mind. The mind must be able to function without hindrance if we are to remain in a healthy state of mind. A healthy mind helps bring about a healthy body. The thoughts are healthy; feelings are healthy. Feeling healthy is also attributed to a healthy mind. Understanding of any type requires a healthy mind. How can one understand if the mind isn't functioning normally?

In the Book of Isaiah 26:3 (King James Version)

Thou will keep him in perfect peace, whose mind is stayed on thee: because he trusteth in thee.

Philippians 2:5 *(King James Version)* Let this mind be in you, which was also in Christ Jesus. What was the mind of Christ? The mind of truth. Christ's mind was and still is the Truth of God. He did not come to make a name for himself, but He came to do the will of God. Why is it so important to be Christ-like in our minds?

St John 8:32 *(King James Version)*

And ye shall know the truth, and the truth shall make you free. Jesus is the truth, and let no man deceive you by any means that He is not. The mind is like the control base or headquarters for everything in our body. Pain, sorrow, joy, happiness, anger, sickness, and such passes through the mind for processing. Our ability to learn, whether by experience or being taught by someone, is processed in our minds. So, as the mind is critical to our physical body, our spiritual mind is to our spiritual man. The poison is aimed at our mind to reject what God has for us in His Kingdom. If we don't protect our spiritual man, our physical man will also be destroyed. We must protect our mind by having the helmet of salvation, which the Apostle Paul speaks about when describing the whole armor of God, which exhorts us to put it on.

Ephesians 6:10 *(King James Version)*

1) Helmets protect our heads, which house our minds. Your spiritual helmet will protect your spiritual mind. We must put on the whole armor of God to stand against the wiles of the devil. Oh, how we could keep a healthy mind if we protected it! God, in His infinite wisdom, provides us with all we need to survive the onslaught of our minds.

2) The Heart

Again, referring to Webster's Dictionary, the heart is (a) the hollow muscular organ that receives and pumps blood throughout the body and (b) the center or innermost part of a place. It is also considered the center or source of emotions and personality attributes.

Wow, now this is an amazing and vital organ. It's hollow but muscular. It pumps and receives blood throughout our body. Blood is the very substance needed to sustain life in our bodies. Life is in the blood, and without it, we would die. So, the heart pumps life through our body and is also the center of source of our emotions and personality. Have you ever heard the saying of a coldhearted or warmhearted individual? Yes, we harbor different emotions in our hearts. It may be hollow, but it's not empty. This is the same place where Jesus wants to live, in our hearts. Just like the blood gives us life, Jesus gives us eternal life when He lives in our hearts.

The heart is a muscle that needs to be exercised. This muscle is used in the pumping action. Jesus will exercise truth so that we may be set free from sin. We protect the heart by putting on the breastplate of righteousness. We need a healthy heart. Physical exercise, eating healthy foods, and regular checkups ensure that our heart is kept in a healthy state.

In the same spiritual sense, by fasting, praying, reading, and studying God's Word, we can maintain a healthy heart for our spiritual man. When we fail to maintain healthy hearts, we open portals for heart disease, heart failure, and other diseases that, little by little, destroy our hearts. Diseases are the same as poisons. They go unnoticed because we become too busy with the cares of this world and not maintaining a spiritually healthy lifestyle. We tend to blame everything and everyone else for our failure, but the bottom line is that it's our heart, and we must make time to keep it healthy. No one else is responsible for our health.

The same holds when we neglect God's Word or His calling in our lives. We ignore God, and our soul/spirit becomes restless, lonely, and desperate because the cares of this world overcome and consume us. We become so desperate in our souls that we accept what sounds right, but because we have no Truth in us, we can't discern the truth from lies. Protect your heart. Receive Jesus as a forever tenant or resident inside of your heart.

Jesus Himself declared in **Revelation 3:20-22**

Behold, I stand at the door and knock: if any man hears my voice and opens the door, I will come into him and sup with him, and he with me. To him that overcometh will I grant to sit with me in my throne, even as I also overcame, and am set down with my Father in his throne.

He that hath an ear, let him hear what the Spirit saith unto the churches.

ARE YOU LISTENING? OUR SEED: **Proverbs 22:6**

Train up a child in the way he should go, and when he is old, he will not depart from it. The poisoning starts early in our lives.

~CHAPTER 7~
A FALLING AWAY

The Apostle Paul, when writing to the church in **Thessalonians, warns in II Thessalonians, 2nd chapter verses 1-3**

Now we beseech you, brethren, by the coming of our Lord Jesus teaches Christ, and by our gathering together unto him,

That ye be not soon shaken in mind, or be troubled, neither by Spirit, nor by word, nor by letter as from us, as that the day of Christ is at hand.

Let no man deceive you by any means: for that day shall not come, except there comes a falling away first, and that man of sin be revealed, the son of perdition.

Paul warns us of the poison to come yet admonishes us not to be shaken in mind or

Spirit about the things to come. This poison will deceive many into turning away from God and following false prophets, liars, deceivers, and those who are contrary and against God. Jesus speaks in **St Matthew 24:24**

24 For there shall arise false Christs, and false prophets, and shall shew great signs and wonders; insomuch that, if it were possible, they shall deceive the very elect. False prophets, false Christ, showing great signs and wonders, causing many to turn away from the truth. We, as true believers of God, have no business following after signs because the signs will follow them that believe.

St Mark 16: 15-18

And he said unto them, go ye into all the world, and preach the gospel to every creature.

He that believeth and is baptized shall be saved; but he that believeth not shall be damned.

And these signs shall follow them that believe; In my name shall they cast out devils; they shall speak with new tongues:

They shall take up serpents; and if they drink any deadly thing, it shall not hurt them; they shall lay hands on the sick, and they shall recover.

Jesus, during His time in Ministry, didn't look for signs and wonders to perform miracles. The signs and wonders followed everywhere He went. Time after time, the signs followed Him, and the signs testified of God's wondrous works. For Jesus came not to do His will but the will of His Father. Not only did the signs follow Him, but the people also followed, trying to catch a glimpse of Him. They followed because the signs and wonders followed Jesus. They followed because many needed to be healed and delivered, both physically, mentally, and spiritually. They needed to be set free from the bondages that came from the cares of this world. Jesus rebuked all kinds of evil spirits from them, and they were made free: mind, body, and soul. Poison can inflict damage to the mind, body, and soul. Jesus walked through the cities and healed them that needed healing. He didn't discriminate from person to person. Where there was a need, Jesus filled it.

The Bible teaches about the falling away of His people. A falling away from the truth. The poison of deceitfulness will cause many with itching ears to fall away. Jesus, in the parable of the Sowers, describes some as falling upon stony places where there was no depth to which they could grasp and grow. Preachers who don't preach the unadulterated Word of God are like these Sowers that allow the seeds to fall into Stoney places. A good Sower will Sow in good ground where the soil has been tilled and prepared for the seeds to be planted. A place where the seeds will receive all the nutrients, water, sun, and freedom to grow.

Just like a shepherd, a Sower must treat his work as unto the Lord. To whom much is given, much is required. The seeds that fell in Stoney places had no chance to become rooted and grounded in the earth because they had no place for their roots to secure themselves. We, as saved people, must seek out the truth. It may require us to dig into the depths of the Word of God, where we can become rooted and grounded. God cursed the ground, but the Sower must till the earth and always sow in good ground. We must seek out the depths of Truth in God's Word, which requires studying. Always pray before reading God's Word and ask Him for knowledge, understanding, and wisdom. When we earnestly pray and are hungry for His Word, He will open the television of our mind and show us His Word coming alive within us. God's word living in us prevents any poisons from entering and destroying us, mind, body, and soul.

~CHAPTER 8~
TYPES OF POISONINGS

We know that there are many types of poisonings in our world that can cause sickness, diseases, paralytic conditions, and even death. God has blessed man to identify these poisons and their effects on mankind. Man has been taught to seek out a counteraction to the poisons through different antidotes to slow down or prevent the poisoning from reaching its full effect on the vital organs in our bodies. The agency called upon when there are questions concerning poisons is the Center for Disease Control (CDC). We also have a spiritual CDC, better known as The Holy Spirit. These poisons that I speak of are spiritual poisons that enter one's mind and seek to destroy the spiritual brain cells.

In Galatians 5:19-21 *(King James Version)*

Now the works of the flesh are manifest, which are these; Adultery, fornication, uncleanness, lasciviousness,

Idolatry, witchcraft, hatred, variance, emulations, wrath, strife, seditions, heresies, 21 Envyings, murders, drunkenness, revellings, and such like: of the which I tell you before, as I have also told you in time past, that they which do such things shall not inherit the kingdom of God.

James 4:4 *(King James Version)*

4 Ye adulterers and adulteresses, know ye not that the friendship of the world is enmity with God? Whosoever, therefore, will be a friend of the world is the enemy of God.

Hebrews 13:4 *(King James Version)*

4 Marriage is honourable in all, and the bed undefiled: but whoremongers and adulterers God will judge.

I Corinthians 6:9-11 *(King James Version)*

Know ye not that the unrighteous shall not inherit the kingdom of God? Be not deceived: neither fornicators, nor idolaters, nor adulterers, nor effeminate, nor abusers of themselves with mankind, Nor thieves, nor covetous, nor drunkards, nor revilers, nor extortioners, shall inherit the kingdom of God.

And such were some of you: but ye are washed, but ye are sanctified, but ye are justified in the name of the Lord Jesus, and by the Spirit of our God.

Many more scriptures teach us about poisons and how to prevent them from entering our bodies, both physical and spiritual. These are only a few to steer you to study for yourself and seek out physical and spiritual remedies because only you know what you're dealing with on the inside.

~CHAPTER 9~
NOTHING TO DO WITH SALVATION

ST MATTHEW 28:17-20

And when they saw him, they worshipped him: but some doubted.

And Jesus came and spake unto them, saying, All power is given unto me in heaven and in earth.

Go ye therefore, and teach all nations, baptizing them in the name of the Father, and of the Son, and of the Holy Ghost:

Teaching them to observe all things whatsoever I have commanded you: and, lo, I am with you always, even unto the end of the world. Amen.

THE BOOK OF ACTS 2: 14-44

But Peter, standing up with the eleven, lifted up his voice, and said unto them, Ye men of Judaea, and all ye that dwell at Jerusalem, be this known unto you, and hearken to my words:

For these are not drunken, as ye suppose, seeing it is but the third hour of the day.

But this is that which was spoken by the prophet Joel;

And it shall come to pass in the last days, saith God, I will pour out of my Spirit upon all flesh: and your sons and your daughters shall prophesy, and your young men shall see visions, and your old men shall dream dreams: And on my servants and on my handmaidens I will pour out in those days of my Spirit; and they shall prophesy:

And I will shew wonders in heaven above, and signs in the earth beneath; blood, and fire, and vapour of smoke:

The sun shall be turned into darkness, and the moon into blood, before the great and notable day of the Lord come:

And it shall come to pass, that whosoever shall call on the name of the Lord shall be saved.

Ye men of Israel, hear these words; Jesus of Nazareth, a man approved of God among you by miracles and wonders and signs, which God did by him in the midst of you, as ye yourselves also know:

Him, being delivered by the determinate counsel and foreknowledge of God, ye have taken, and by wicked hands have crucified and slain:

Whom God hath raised up, having loosed the pains of death: because it was not possible that he should be holden of it.

For David speaketh concerning him, I foresaw the Lord always before my face, for he is on my right hand, that I should not be moved:

Therefore, did my heart rejoice, and my tongue was glad; moreover, also my flesh shall rest in hope:

Because thou wilt not leave my soul in hell, neither wilt thou suffer thine Holy One to see corruption.

Thou hast made known to me the ways of life; thou shalt make me full of joy with thy countenance.

Men and brethren, let me freely speak unto you of the patriarch David, that he is both dead and buried, and his sepulchre is with us unto this day. Therefore, being a prophet, and knowing that God had sworn with an oath to him, that of the fruit of his loins, according to the flesh, he would raise up Christ to sit on his throne;

He seeing this before spake of the resurrection of Christ, that his soul was not left in hell, neither his flesh did see corruption.

This Jesus hath God raised up, whereof we all are witnesses. Therefore, being by the right hand of God exalted and having received of the Father the promise of the Holy Ghost, he hath shed forth this, which ye now see and hear.

For David is not ascended into the heavens: but he saith himself, The Lord said unto my Lord, sit thou on my right hand, 35 Until I make thy foes thy footstool.

Therefore, let all the house of Israel know assuredly, that God hath made the same Jesus, whom ye have crucified, both Lord and Christ.

Now when they heard this, they were pricked in their heart, and said unto Peter and to the rest of the apostles, Men, and brethren, what shall we do? Then Peter said unto them, Repent, and be baptized every one of you in the name of Jesus Christ for the remission of sins, and ye shall receive the gift of the Holy Ghost. For the promise is unto you, and to your children, and to all that are afar off, even as many as the Lord our God shall call.

And with many other words did he testify and exhort, saying, Save yourselves from this untoward generation.

Then they that gladly received his word were baptized: and the same day there were added unto them about three thousand souls.

And they continued steadfastly in the apostles' doctrine and fellowship, and in breaking of bread, and in prayers.

And fear came upon every soul: and many wonders and signs were done by the apostles.

And all that believed were together and had all things common.

This chapter shows Jesus's instructions as He commissioned the disciples into The Apostleship. He told them to go and teach all nations, baptizing them in the name of The Father, Son, and Holy Ghost. Teaching them to observe whatsoever things I have commanded you. The things that Jesus commanded to be taught, even this commandment, have been poisoned to the point that the teachings in some churches are teaching everything but that. Jesus taught about Love, Obedience, Faithfulness, Gentleness, and all of the fruits of the Spirit. Yet, because of the poisoning of the minds of many, we've slowly gone away from the True teachings of Christ. Traditions that have nothing to do with salvation have crept onto the pulpit unawares simply because they may have sound good but not sound doctrine, looked good but not Holy, felt good but not of love, and even the term of a "new revelation," gives the hearers a sense of something spectacular is about to be revealed. However:

Ecclesiastes 1:9

The thing that hath been, it is that which shall be, and that which is done is that which shall be done: and there is no new thing under the sun.

For the popularity vote, we sometimes think that if we use this "New Revelation" quote, our wisdom status will increase to those who are listening to us. But God is listening, and we must account for all those words we use out of context to appear more knowledgeable and impressionable to others. This thinking only leads to a prideful spirit and a deceitful heart. It looks Holy and profound but has no roots in Holiness, like the seeds planted by the wayside, amongst the thorns, and on stony grounds (mainly in the stony heart). And this same poison begins to poison those who have no study habits and look to depend on their leaders to direct them in Truth. Little do they realize that you're being poisoned and deceived. They also must give an account of not seeking God for themselves. Any leader that teaches or implies that only through their teachings and doctrines can one obtain salvation is teaching in error. This must stop!

Each one of us must be responsible for seeking out our salvation. Traditional teachings are just that, traditions passed on from generation to generation. THE BUCK MUST STOP SOMEWHERE! Be the one who says,

"ENOUGH IS ENOUGH!

These teachings that we're the only TRUE CHURCH is poison.

1 Corinthians 13:8-10 (King James Version)

Charity never faileth: but whether there be prophecies, they shall fail; whether there be tongues, they shall cease; whether there be knowledge, it shall vanish away. For we know in part, and we prophesy in part.

But when that which is perfect is come, then that which is in part shall be done away.

Money, clergy apparel, buildings, popularity, community influence, robes, jewelry, artifacts, and so on have nothing to do with salvation. See **St John 3:16** and understand it.

~CHAPTER 10~

TYPES OF INOCULATIONS

verb (used with object), in·oc·u·lat·ed, in·oc·u·lat·ing.
to implant (a disease agent or antigen) in a person, animal, or plant to produce a disease for study or to stimulate disease resistance.

To affect or treat (a person, animal, or plant) in this manner.

To introduce (microorganisms) into surroundings suited to their growth as a culture medium.

To imbue (a person), as with ideas.

Metallurgy. to treat (molten metal) chemically to strengthen the microstructure.

These are the definitions given by dictionary.com for the meaning of inoculation. As you can see, the definitions are not favorable to good health. On the spiritual, it operates by the same principles. However, there are many methods to achieve inoculations. The main one is vaccination. Yes, with a needle that pierces the skin and injects the poison into the bloodstream. Once inside the bloodstream, it causes damaging effects on the entire body by destabilizing one or many of its organs, which are vital for survival. The heart, lungs, liver, pancreas, brain, kidneys, stomach, and intestines. Each of these organs is vital for survival. One goes down, and it will begin to cause the others to overwork to make up for the lost one, but because of their design, they cannot effectively compensate. Our adversary does not care how the poison is administered just as long as it gets into the spiritual bloodstream and causes.

THE BLOOD COVERING OF JESUS to become contaminated, rendering it ineffective against the wiles of the devil. He uses:

FALSE APOSTLES
FALSE PROPHETS
FALSE PASTORS
FALSE EVANGELISTS
FALSE TEACHERS
FALSE BISHOPS
FALSE DOCTRINES
FALSE ANOINTING

We all must do our part to protect ourselves from:

THE CHURCH OF THE POISONED MIND

BE AND STAY BLESSED........

~EPILOGUE~

I want to take time out to, first and foremost, thank God for leading and guiding me through the writing of this book, which has been a blessing. I pray that something was said to provoke you to recognize the poisons and their remedies. This book is to encourage individuals to realize the times we're living in and to seek out their own soul salvation in Christ Jesus, for the time will come and is now when they will not endure sound doctrine.

Blessings to all and Love Eternal.

www.ingramcontent.com/pod-product-compliance
Lightning Source LLC
Chambersburg PA
CBHW041926090426
42743CB00020B/3456